ROTHERHAM PUBLIC LIBRARIES

This book must be returned by the latest date entered above.
The loan may be extended [personally, by post or telephone]
for a further period if the book is not required by another reader.

LMI

A DORLING KINDERSLEY BOOK

Written by Angela Royston
Editor Mary Ling
Art Editor Nigel Hazle
Production Louise Barratt
Illustrator Rowan Clifford

First published in Great Britain in 1992 by
Dorling Kindersley Limited, 9 Henrietta Street, London WC2E 8PS

A CIP catalogue record for this book is available
from the British Library

ISBN 0-86318-681-5

Colour reproduction by J. Film Process Ltd, Singapore
Printed in Italy by L.E.G.O.

SEE HOW THEY GROW

MOUSE

photographed by
BARRIE WATTS

DORLING KINDERSLEY
London • New York • Stuttgart

Just arrived

I have just been born.
I cannot see or hear.
I have no fur to
keep me warm.

I snuggle in a
cosy nest with my
brothers and sisters.

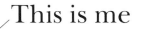

This is me

This is our mother. She is
coming to feed us her milk.
We are very hungry.

Out of the nest

I am two days old. Fine black
hair is growing over my pink skin.
My eyes and ears are still closed.

Where am I?
I am lost.

I squeak as loud as I can until my
mother hears me. She will carry me home.

My first crawl

I am two weeks old. My eyes
are open. At last I can see
and hear. I can walk too.

My mother watches
me as I explore. I sniff
everything I find.

Now I am going
back to my nest for
a nap. It has been
an exciting day.

Playing in a flowerpot

I am three weeks old. My claws are sharp and my legs are getting strong.

I am playing in this flowerpot, but the walls are slippery. Help! The pot is rolling away.

From here,
I can see all
around me.

Look! My sister is
peeping out of
another flowerpot.

Looking after ourselves

Now I am four weeks old.
I spend most of the
time with my brothers and sisters.

We like to play together.

Then I clean myself. My long tail needs special care.

Climbing high

I am six weeks old and
I am growing stronger.
My brothers, sisters
and I have climbed
this branch.

We cling on to the thin branches with our claws.

Our long tails help us to balance.

Finding food

Now I am eight weeks old. I enjoy finding my own food.

I sniff and twitch my nose when I smell nice things to eat.

My favourite food is grain. I hold it between my paws. I nibble it with my long front teeth.

See how I grew

Newborn

Two days old

Two weeks old

Three weeks old

Four weeks old

Six weeks old

Eight weeks old

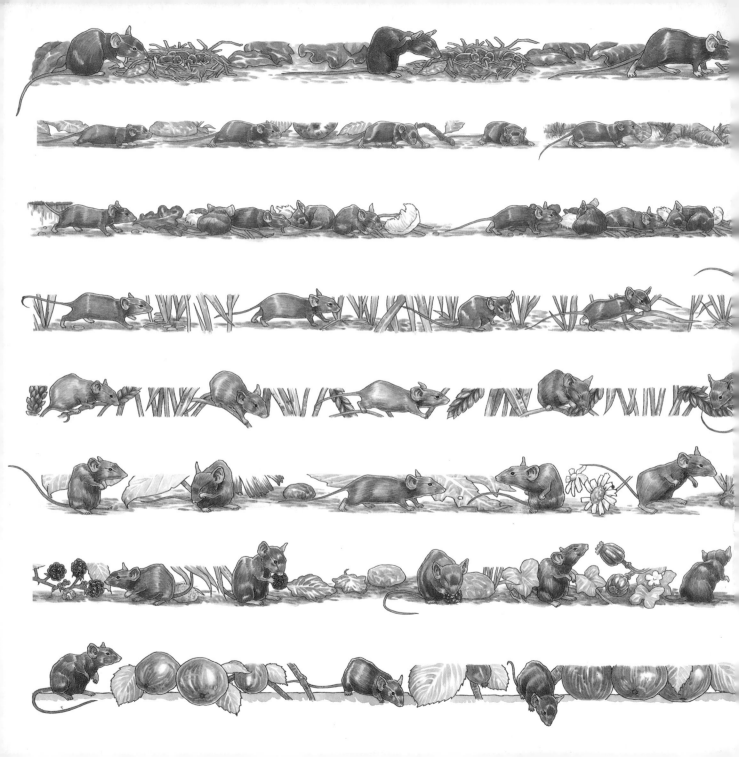